21 DAYS
BACK
TO GOD

The most significant day in the life of every Christian is our Baptismal Day, when we are commissioned and anointed as Disciples of the Risen Jesus and given the gift of Eternity.

Being a Disciple of Jesus is the greatest gift that can be given to any person; it is a call to be an intimate friend of Jesus and to grasp his unconditional love. The journey of every disciple is full of the unknown and it does require total trust in the Lord and, usually, mountains to be climbed and oceans to be crossed. On the journey, times of great light and darkness.

All the way through the journey of life the Lord will be by our side. And as we discover from this honest and open account, the Lord has guided Bob Cameron every step of the way on his personal pilgrimage of return.

Bishop Terry Brady,
Auxiliary Bishop Emeritus of Sydney.

This is a delightful and very honest book. It's full of practical steps anyone, but especially an older lapsed Catholic, can take back to the truth and joy of the faith. Bob Cameron tells his story with clarity and love, clearly overjoyed to be safely back home in the Church he once stormed out of in rage. It's a story we can all get behind.

Dr Philippa Martyr,
Academic and Catholic Weekly columnist.

This is an authentic personal account of a person, who like many others, lost his way in the cultural and religious amnesia of the twentieth century. It tells the poignant, moving story of how he found his way back, after many decades, and recognised the spiritual home base he had always sought. Bob Cameron's story is a poignant, sensitive and engaging journey which will resonate with young and older readers, with not only with Catholics but all spiritual seekers who yearn for something beyond this world.

Wanda Skowronska, PhD.
Psychologist and author, Sydney.

AFTER FORTY YEARS OF RUNNING AWAY
A PILGRIMAGE OF RETURN

21 DAYS BACK TO GOD

BOB CAMERON

Published in Australia by
Coventry Press
33 Scoresby Road
Bayswater VIC 3153

ISBN 9781922589262

Copyright © Bob Cameron 2023

All rights reserved. Other than for the purposes and subject to the conditions prescribed under the *Copyright Act*, no part of this publication may be reproduced, stored in a retrieval system, or transmitted in any form or by any means, electronic, mechanical, photocopying, recording or otherwise, without the prior permission of the publisher.

Nihil Obstat:	Reverend Gerard Diamond MA (Oxon), LSS, D.Theol.
	Diocesan Censor
Imprimatur:	Very Reverend Joseph Caddy AM Lic.Soc.Sci VG
	Vicar General
	Archdiocese of Melbourne
Date:	17 November 2022

The Nihil Obstat and Imprimatur are official declarations that a book or pamphlet is free of doctrinal or moral error. No implication is contained therein that those who have granted the Nihil Obstat and Imprimatur agree with the contents, opinions or statements expressed. They do not necessarily signify that the work is approved as a basic text for catechetical instruction.

Catalogue-in-Publication entry is available from the National Library of Australia
http://catalogue.nla.gov.au

Cover design by Ian James – www.jgd.com.au
Text design by Coventry Press
Set in EB Garamond

Printed in Australia

Contents

Foreword ... 7

Introduction ... 9

21 Days ... 13

Day 1
Make the Sign of the Cross – it could change your life ... 15

Day 2
Say a prayer – and make your soul sit-up ... 17

Day 3
Say hello to Jesus ... 19

Day 4
Jogging with Jesus ... 21

Day 5
The old 's' word ... 23

Day 6
Doubt is the grit of faith ... 25

Day 7
A time of reflection ... 27

Day 8
The power of parables ... 29

Day 9
Time to knock on the door? ... 31

Day 10
Two forgotten rules of the road   33

Day 11
Heavenly checklist   35

Day 12
A child again   38

Day 13
A dip in the deep end with God   40

Day 14
Take the weight off your souls   43

Day 15
The bread of life   45

Day 16
Give God a second chance   47

Day 17
Saints with battered haloes   49

Day 18
A matter of choice   52

Day 19
True confessions   54

Day 20
No lightning bolts from the pulpit   58

Day 21
Back to the future   61

Foreword

Those interested in finding a persuasive case for embracing and living Catholic faith, or another form of Christian faith, do not lack valuable books to read. Earlier authors have become classics in this area. I think of such writers as St John Henry Newman, G. K. Chesterton, T. S. Eliot, Dorothy Sayers, and Flannery O'Connor. Nowadays the works of Rowan Williams and others, including Christopher Jamison (e.g. *Finding the Language of Grace*), fill this need.

Bob Cameron offers something more personal, in fact, intensely personal, in his guide for 'collapsed' Catholics yearning to return to the faith. He does this as a 'spiritual refugee who has made the journey' after 'forty years of running away'.

After a 'chastening encounter in the Confessional Box', he stormed out of the church, and at the age of eighteen 'went into voluntary exile'. He entered, as he puts it, 'a state of spiritual amnesia' for more than three decades.

In the vivid language of a fine journalist, Bob tells his story of 'making a personal connection' again with God.

He does this through a scheme of twenty-one days: Day One: 'Make the Sign of the Cross – it could change your life'; Day Two: 'Say a prayer – and make your soul sit up'; Day Three: 'Say hello to Jesus'; and so forth.

Bob brilliantly evokes what he felt after deciding to attend Mass at the Cathedral of Notre Dame in Paris. He also conveys a wonderful sense of what it was like to enter a parish church after years away, and experience 'the living presence of Jesus in the tabernacle' – 'Jesus is patiently waiting there for anyone who'd like to visit for a chat. No appointment necessary.'

The climax of Bob's return from exile of forty years came when he decided to go back to confession. An attempt to make a general confession was thwarted by an angry priest. At home that evening, he decided to google God and typed in the search box: 'Just tried to re-join Catholic Church by going to confession. Priest not helpful. What can I do?'

Pages of results emerged within seconds. Bob added: 'If you type in a version of that question today, you will get almost 17 million results in 0.62 seconds'. Back then, 'the suggested links covered just about everything anyone needs to know about confession'.

'It took me', Bob recalled 'an hour or two to find a response that gave the guidance I needed. A post by a blogger revealed a similar encounter with a priest, but said he later found one who answered his prayers'. Bob tells movingly the story of the welcoming help he received from this 'rescue-priest'.

This is a beautifully modest book that keeps well away from self-indulgence. It evokes a brilliant picture of the Catholic Church as Bob left and as he found it again, forty years later. The whole story is pervaded by a sense of truth and forgiving love. I cannot recommend too highly this guide for returning refugees.

Gerald O'Collins, SJ. AC

Fr Gerald O'Collins, professor emeritus of the Gregorian University (Rome), has authored or co-authored 81 books. His latest work, with Nevie Peters, is *Letters from the Pandemic* (Brisbane: Connor Court Publishing, 2022).

Introduction

A personal guide for 'collapsed' Catholics
yearning to return to the faith
by a spiritual refugee who has made the journey.

Most Catholics do not recall the most important day of their lives: their entry into the faith through baptism as infants. But it is probable that many non-practising Catholics remember only too well the day they quit the Church. I clearly recall storming out the door of my city's cathedral after a chastening encounter in the Confessional Box. I left without a second thought and went into voluntary exile. I was angry with priests trying to control my life and asking too many questions. I had not understood that most of them were just trying to do their job.

I was 18 and part of the Great Flight of the Sixties and millions more have since taken the same well-beaten path away from our ancient religion. Runaways do not need a map; I simply ran until I entered a state of spiritual amnesia for more than three decades. I became a 'collapsed' Catholic.

By the time I reached forty, I was a senior media executive and happily married with two children. As a journalist, I had lived through many experiences, including a last-minute rescue from being shot dead in a city where – historically – people killed each other in the name of God. But not once during that grim night in a Belfast alley did my thoughts or thanks turn to that same God. I believed my destiny was in my own hands, or the pay packet of whichever media baron was hiring my services.

Then, unexpectedly, in my fifties, I began to feel a yearning, a stirring in my heart for something I could not quite pin down. It was several years before I began to accept it was the God spark still flickering in my rusty old soul. An unspoken urge was drawing me to retrace my steps to the door I had slammed shut so many years before.

But unlike escapees, 'returnees' do need a map because I could not find the right path back. I had forgotten The Way. I had lost my moral compass. And, oddly, for someone who earned a living making dozens of decisions a day, I could not bring myself to just knock on the door of the local parish priest and ask for the directions 'home.' All I had to say was that I was a returnee – a comeback Catholic – and ask what I should do next. But I could not bring myself to do it.

I felt guilty and ashamed. I had broken too many rules on countless occasions, not the least missing Sunday Mass over two thousand times for the past forty years. I just did not have the courage to ask for help by a priest or those I knew to be practising Catholics. Finally, it dawned on me that there was someone I could ask for help. Someone non-judgmental, kind, wise and always ready to share the load, in short, the perfect confidante: God. My soul may have been barnacle encrusted, but I did remember from childhood being taught to have an open dialogue with Jesus, that is chat with him. So began my interior pilgrimage back to the Church, a journey from which I would draw great solace, strength and knowledge from the Godman who died and rose again to save us all, Jesus of Nazareth. And he treated this spiritual refugee with nothing but the compassion of the Good Samaritan.

I know from personal experience that more than a few non-practising Catholics have similar reservations and anxieties about returning to the faith we once shared. It is why I have written this guide – to share the steps that helped me find the way back to our spiritual home. I am no longer young, but I feel what I have written holds true for any age or stage. There is no need to follow every step, of course, this *Prodigal Son* took the long way home. The inner light of your faith may well shine on a shorter path back

Introduction

to God. It could depend on how hungry your soul is. But this is how I made my Pilgrimage of Return.

21 DAYS

21 DAYS

DAY 1

MAKE THE SIGN OF THE CROSS – IT COULD CHANGE YOUR LIFE

Pope Francis calls making this blessing our first and most simple prayer, learnt at our mother or father's knee. I had not thought about this every-day blessing for years. Then one morning while passing my parish church I saw a young woman pause to look intently at the building and make the Sign of the Cross. Not a hurried sketch of the sign, but a reverential salutation to God who silently waits in the tabernacle of every Catholic church the world over.

I'd only recently begun to think about returning to the faith and felt a wave of emotion as I watched her act of devotion. It was a 'Lest we forget' moment and I realised what I had forgotten. I'd forgotten the ancient sign that reminds us of the courageous death and joyful resurrection of Jesus.

I would like to say I followed the young woman's act of homage that day, but I didn't. I was too embarrassed by the idea of making a public display. Besides, I was not a real Catholic, was I? At best, I was a poor counterfeit. But I couldn't get the image of her act of reverence out of my mind. And several days later, when alone in the house, I touched my forehead, lower chest and then each shoulder with my fingertips while silently saying: 'In the name of the Father and of the Son and of the Holy Ghost. Amen'.

I did not then know the Church had exorcised the 'ghost' word and substituted the more sacred 'Spirit.' But the reverential act itself has remained virtually unchanged for more than seventeen hundred years. And in making the Sign that day, I felt I'd taken my first practical step back to the spiritual realm of our Church. I began to feel I was no longer a stranger to God. I was making a personal connection with him again, thanks to observing a young woman practise her faith in such a simple and public way. She may have been a total stranger, but she was certainly a local angel.

> *Make the sign of the cross before you go to sleep tonight – it could change your life*

SAY A PRAYER –
AND MAKE YOUR SOUL SIT-UP

WHEN WAS THE LAST time you said an honest-to-God prayer? I have few powers of retention when it comes to remembering a line of poetry, the lyrics of a favourite song, or the punch line of a joke. But there are two powerful prayers from my childhood that I have never forgotten. The *Hail Mary* and the *Our Father* or the *Lord's Prayer*. I had not uttered or muttered these two prayers for nearly half a century, but they were still firmly anchored in my mind; written in my heart and imprinted on my soul.

After months of prevaricating about taking the next step back to the faith, I finally felt an overwhelming need to fall on my knees and say a prayer. Any prayer. I chose the *Hail Mary*, the one that tells the story of a single, young girl learning she is to be the mother of God. For me, it is the moment our Church was born, but none of this was on my mind at that moment as I knelt next to my home office desk. I just needed to pray. Although I had no idea what I was praying for. It became the moment of truth for me.

As I knelt and silently prayed, the door opened and in walked my wife. Rosalie is a Belfast-born Protestant but not a rigid thinker. She was aware I'd been developing an interest in alternative religious beliefs for some time. In effect, I'd been wandering in a spiritual maze and avoiding the truth.

I just had not openly expressed a desire to return to Catholicism, a religion I'd roundly criticised for many years. But now, there I was on my knees, hands pressed together palm-to-palm, and my head bowed in prayer. Startled, I looked up to see her slowly backing out and closing the door behind her, an understanding smile lighting her face.

I felt deeply self-conscious but resisted jumping up and rushing after her to try to explain my actions. My heart was lurching wildly, but I finished my prayer and then said the *Our Father*. The foundational psalm of our faith that Jesus taught the Apostles, revealing the loving bond that God wants with us, his family. I made the sign of the cross and stood up and felt an overpowering need to do something more.

Then I realised what it was. I hurried to my wife and said, 'I have got to go into the city. I have got to buy a prayer book'. So, I did and slowly began to nourish my ailing soul back to life.

> *Find a prayer that resonates with you. One that makes the soul sit up and take notice, instead of languishing in a dusty corner with a blanket over its head.*

SAY HELLO TO JESUS

THE NAME JESUS is one of the most uttered words in the world – often as a profanity, and many times as an expression of shock, joy, or a plea for help. It's the word on many a lip, regardless of the speaker being a believer or not. Despite this familiarity, how often do we think about taking the next step and having a wee chat, an interior conversation, with Jesus?

Prayer is one way, of course, whether formal, simple, or just a silent appeal for guidance. But I'm thinking more about the interior dialogue priests urged us to use with God in our childhood, to see him as a steadfast friend we can safely open our hearts to. Or even become angry with.

I am referring to something deeper than that small, inner voice we hear when our conscience is flagging a red alert. Or when we tap into that inner wisdom stored up from a lifetime's experience. I am talking about a silent act, both sacred and quite matter of fact. This understanding slowly dawned on me, as I began to pray regularly again. Renewing my relationship with God, primarily through the human face of Jesus. I remembered how talking to Jesus got me through tough times as a child, giving me strength, comfort and support.

So, one day, I cleared the spiritual vocal cords, scraped off the rust and opened the dialogue with my old friend, Jesus. I did not say or ask for anything ambitious. I apologised for not being in touch for such a long time and asked if we could pick up from where we left off so long ago? From that moment, I put Jesus on speed-dial, and I discuss many things with him. If I wander off track at times, or cannot see the wood for the trees, he will send me 'reminders'. Otherwise known as insights.

This renewed friendship has also given me a sense of peace and been a source of inner strength. One of the greatest gifts of this dialogue has been the slow dissolving of rancour in my heart. It's a different way of praying and deeply renewing.

> *Say hello to Jesus – he will always take your call. And if the line is busy, just leave a message and he will get back to you.*

JOGGING WITH JESUS

AT LEAST ONCE a year, we make a vow to develop good habits, usually to become more fit or healthy. But often we then fall off the proverbial wagon. Maybe the goal we've set is too ambitious. We can expect too much of ourselves or push too hard, too soon. We risk losing heart.

I began light jogging many years ago, long before I had notions of returning to the Church. It was for heart health reasons and, at first light, I'd jog five times around a nearby football field. I also began using the time to try and resolve the problem of the day, be it private or work-related. The exercise cleared my head and strengthened my sense of purpose.

So, when I started wrestling with my re-emerging faith, I began to pray for guidance as I ran. I was now running towards God and not away from him. The dawn jog became a form of meditation. I was rebuilding a relationship, re-integrating God into my life. Or, more accurately, he was bringing me back into his. Over time, I switched to walking as it is more relaxing and medically proven to help lower high blood pressure.

Each morning, I ask Jesus to walk with me and the dialogue continues, often just a simple prayer of thanks, or appealing for strength and direction in dealing with worrying problems. It's sharing the load as he asked us to do when he offered the support of his yoke. He's offering to put his arm around our shoulders. Praying for help is also something many automatically do in moments of danger or deep distress as I now know from experience. Eight years ago, I began to experience a heart attack while jogging. It was just before dawn, and I'd forgotten to bring my 'phone with me. There was nobody nearby to ask for help and as the pain grew worse, I began to walk back to my home about five minutes away. As I walked, I prayed for help. Just a simple plea of 'Jesus, help me'. It focused my mind, and I felt my resolve to survive deepening. My wife drove me to hospital and a medical team saved my life.

I thanked them profusely and, unlike that night in Belfast, I also thanked God with all my newly repaired heart. I also promised the cardiac surgeon that if there is a 'next time', I would dial 000 for an ambulance.

They are crewed by angels of mercy equipped with heart-starting defibrillators.

THE OLD 'S' WORD

'THE ROAD TO HELL is paved with good intentions' declares the old saying. Then, arguably, the road to heaven is cracked and pitted with bad intentions, or sins that have been forgiven. Sin or the 's' word can be a problem for many practising and lapsed Catholics. It smacks of old-style religion, moral judgment, and old-fashioned Catholic guilt. For example, I recently heard a parish elder publicly urging people not to let 'shame, false pride or laziness stop you from going to confession'. And this was to a congregation of regular churchgoers. Her rallying cry rang familiar bells with me as I recalled my early internal struggle with returning to the Church. But the thought of going to 'Reconciliation' (as the sacrament is also known) and listing my catalogue of 'sins' from the past forty years, was a big stumbling block. The idea of confession frightened me, reinforcing my self-judgment that I was a counterfeit Catholic.

As you will learn later, when I finally found the courage to confess all, I experienced a sense of profound peace and love suddenly filling my life. But that was some time down the track. I was not yet ready to take that step.

You may be experiencing similar reservations. You may now have progressed from reverently making the Sign of the Cross, saying a favourite prayer or two and even opening the lines of communication with God. But you're not quite ready yet for a visit to the Reconciliation room. So, maybe relax for a while on God's couch and reflect a little on your life with him.

Expressing contrition for past mistakes is important for healing, but not in a fearful way. We could all do better but do not berate yourself. As priests often say, 'I too am a sinner.' We know we are not perfect – only God is perfect, or spiritually complete. He hates the sin not the sinner.

Perhaps find comfort and strength in the ancient 'Jesus Prayer'. It is basically unforgettable, just 'Lord Jesus Christ, Son of God, have mercy on me a sinner'. Mercy means receiving God's loving forgiveness. Being who he is, God both forgives and forgets. This makes every day a fresh start in the eyes of God.

We just must try to jump those cracks in the pavement.

DAY 6

DOUBT IS THE GRIT OF FAITH

WITHOUT A DOUBT, there will be moments of doubt on the journey home. It is not wrong to doubt. Do not be afraid to question; it is what makes us human. Thomas the Apostle earned the nickname Doubting Thomas after refusing to believe his companions' claims that Jesus had risen from the grave. But all doubt fled from the sceptical Thomas when Jesus appeared and urged the wavering disciple to closely examine his wounds.

This made Thomas very privileged, or as Jesus said: 'Do you believe because you have seen me? Blessed are those who have not seen and yet have come to believe' (John 20:29). Believing in the resurrection is what makes us Christians. He was talking about us.

Jesus was patient and understanding about the scepticism expressed by Thomas. Jesus was no stranger to the disbelief of others, fatally so. The Temple hierarchy dismissed his claims of a shared divinity with God and demanded his execution for blasphemy.

But his closest disciples – men and women – were with Jesus when he miraculously healed the sick and lame; and found faith in him. Most of these same companions were later martyred because they refused to deny that they had witnessed his resurrection and spoken of it far and wide.

This all happened more than 2,000 years ago, of course. What have these ancient struggles with belief to do with your own journey back to the faith? Well, doubt has continued to be the constant companion of Christian belief, especially in the age of science and the demand for concrete evidence of God's existence.

Personally, I believe in the eye-witness accounts of Christ's life and death in the New Testament as taught by the Church for two millennia.

More to the point, nobody has yet presented proof to me that God does not exist. Not even when they say: If there is a God, why does he allow bad things to happen to good people? Or indeed, why does he allow good things to happen to bad people? These are not Acts of God, but of humanity and nature in the raw. The good in the world far outweighs the bad, otherwise we would have vanished from existence long ago. Just consider how we work together to help people in crisis in distant countries or raise funds for total strangers struck by personal disaster.

We mostly look after each other and we freely choose to do so. We are not God-bots but that spark in our soul does reflect his loving nature. As pilgrims in our daily quest for spiritual conversion, we nurture that ember. Questioning helps us better understand what we are seeking. The answers will come from the heart. Doubt is the grit of faith; it produces pearls of wisdom.

We need to listen for those pearls.

DAY 7

A TIME OF REFLECTION

It's the end of Week One and maybe long-frozen spiritual practices have begun to thaw. Perhaps you are now making the Sign of Cross at times; possibly saying morning or night prayers. You may even have begun silently talking with Jesus, sharing some of your concerns and hopes. There is no rush, God is patient, and we should be too. A time of reflection is important as shown by C S Lewis, famed author of *The Lion, the Witch and the Wardrobe*. He was an atheist until the age of 34 when he suddenly converted to Christianity on a day trip to Whipsnade Zoo in England.

In his book, *Surprised by Joy*, Lewis reveals that his conversion happened after several years of much thought and a long conversation with his Catholic friend, J. R. Tolkien, author of *The Hobbit*. Belfast-born Lewis, a senior Oxford academic, writes: 'I know very well when, but hardly how, the final step was taken. I was driven to Whipsnade one sunny morning. When we set out, I did not believe that Jesus Christ is the Son of God, and when we reached the zoo, I did'.

You may be wondering what a famous author's conversion story has to do with you. Well, faith can be a fragile flower. Every day is a conversion day, even for practising Catholics, because practice helps our faith become more complete. Lewis notes he knew when but 'hardly how' his final step to conversion was taken. It was a mystery to him, perhaps even more so considering he was not kneeling in a church pew but on a day trip to the zoo.

Perhaps it means we don't choose the moment, so much as God chooses when to make the call for spiritual conversion. But, almost certainly, you will know. The impulse is unmistakable and could come when you least expect it, as happened with C.S. Lewis.

As happened with me when the call to return finally came.

DAY 8

THE POWER OF PARABLES

EVEN IF OUR faith has been slumbering for a while, many of us will recall favourite teaching stories – parables – from Sunday Mass during our childhood. *The Good Samaritan* and *The Prodigal Son* are two examples that spring easily to mind. These can provide a rich source of spiritual reflection as we retrace our steps back to God. They are found, of course, in the *Holy Bible*, specifically in the pages of the *New Testament*.

Priests often recommend reading the more familiar *New Testament* first with its four Gospels by Matthew, Mark, Luke and John. Each evangelist provides their own faith-renewing insights into the life-death-and-resurrection of the God-man Jesus Christ. The *New Testament* also contains the illuminating letters of St Paul and vivid accounts of the peril-filled evangelising missions of the Apostles. As well as highlighting the completion of *Old Testament* prophecies of the arrival of the Messiah on earth. But above all, the *New Testament* is a spiritual guide. The primary source of what Jesus was trying to show and tell us about eternal life with God.

In many ways, it is a love story like no other. It is the foundation story of our faith. It can be read online or bought from a Catholic bookshop, whether web based or in a bricks-and-mortar store. The Bible can also be found in local libraries, or perhaps a relative or friend may have a copy somewhere in their home. It's very rare for a Bible to be thrown out – even a one-time, faith-faded character such as myself was fearful of upsetting God by recycling his book.

But you may wonder – which Gospel do I read first? Perhaps a deeply insightful and gripping Gospel to begin with is the chronicle written by Luke, who wrote his account of the life of Christ for a friend called Theophilus. His name means 'friend of God' or 'loved by God' and Theophilus may have been a potential convert to the then tiny but emerging faith of Christianity.

The two parables mentioned above and many others – such as the *Lost Sheep* and *Lazarus and the Rich Man* – are found in Luke's account of Christ. In the eyes of Jesus, the latter parable shows material success on earth is no guarantee of spiritual reward in heaven. The basis of prayers such as the *Hail Mary* and the *Our Father* are also found in Luke's pages, and he has a strong focus on Jesus' deep concern for the poor and marginalised.

Luke, said to have been a doctor, is believed to have written the *Acts of the Apostles* too. *Acts* tells of the struggles and dangers faced by the closest friends of Jesus – and their male and female converts – as they sowed the seeds of Christianity in many parts of the Roman Empire.

Three hundred years later, these seeds bore fruit when the empire converted to Christianity and the universal (catholic) Church was born. The Romans abandoned their many gods for the one God. More than 1,600 years on, you are reading the same words they heard and perhaps feeling what they felt. A connection is being made.

There is much to meet spiritual hunger in the library of God

TIME TO KNOCK ON THE DOOR?

MY FATHER DIED suddenly from a heart attack in England just a few weeks after I arrived in Sydney as a Ten Pound Pom. I'd migrated with my wife and three-year-old daughter, and I didn't have the money to fly home for dad's funeral. Nor did I go into a church to pray for his soul or for mum and my young brother and five sisters.

Instead, on the day of his funeral, I sat on a bench in Sydney's Hyde Park in the shadow of St Mary's Cathedral. I could not bring myself to walk thirty metres to the door of the church and seek solace under the mantle of God. I was so close. But my pride would not let me take that step. My legs were as frozen as my soul.

Many years later, when my resistance began to melt, I 'knocked on the door' of my parish church and stepped into its comforting silence. I was making an exploratory visit. It was on a weekday morning, and I was yearning to know what it felt like to be back in the presence of God. There was only him and me there, and I knew he was at home because of the soft red light flickering near the altar. The light means the consecrated Eucharist, the living presence of Jesus, is in the tabernacle, that little house of God found in the sanctuary of all Catholic churches. Jesus is patiently waiting there for anyone who'd like to visit for a chat. No appointment necessary.

I was not yet ready to talk to a priest or attend Mass. But I wanted to familiarise myself with a church again. To sit quietly in a pew and take it all in once more. It was a sort of retreat, and my guide was unseen. There was the altar now situated so that the priest faces the congregation and no longer has his back to us. There was the familiar font where it all begins with our baptism;

the confessional, the honesty box in which we open our hearts to God. And around the walls of the church hung the 14 Stations of the Cross, marking the last steps of Jesus as a man on earth.

I stayed wrapped in the comforting silence for twenty minutes and then, for the first time in forty years, I said a prayer for my father's soul in a church. I also said a silent prayer of thanks to God for listening to me, blessed myself with the holy water from the font in the porch and closed the door quietly behind me. I no longer felt a total stranger. The old place felt just the same, but I was seeing it with new eyes. For many years, I had told myself that I had rejected the Church but not my belief in God. I was beginning to realise that the Church is the faith, that one cannot truly exist without the other.

I still couldn't bring myself to fully commit to the Church though, perhaps too much water had flowed under the bridge. This is how I felt at the time. You may feel differently after knocking on the door. You might not want to leave again. Still unsure, I was reluctant to linger.

Or perhaps God didn't feel I was ready to make the commitment.

TWO FORGOTTEN RULES OF THE ROAD

WHEN I LEFT the Church at 18, I felt I was being suffocated by the Church's red tape. I was a typical teenage rebel in the New Age of Rebellion, the Sixties. My anthem lay in the sound and lyrics of the Beatles not the dirges slumbering in a dusty old hymnbook. I wanted to exercise my free will without being hounded by God's cops prying into my every thought and action. I wanted to live by my own moral code, and I did for many years. I tied myself up in my own red tape. Living by a dubious code of conduct, largely based on instinct, pride and greed for success. I had convinced myself it was the only way for me. I'd known poverty as a child; and I didn't want to be poor again.

But now I was spiritually poor; and fear, shame and my ego prevented me from making a simple U-turn. I wanted God to give me a reason to reverse direction. Nothing too life-changing, though. But I did not want to be a hypocrite either. I did not want to pay lip service to God. I wanted to have a genuine friendship with him. What was blocking me? I was drowning in confusion and questions that seemingly had no answers.

What was it about the Church's rules and regulations that so angered me all those years ago? What was so unfair about them? Did I even truly know them? I more-or-less knew the Ten Commandments and they were straightforward. I had no argument with them. They're foundational to our justice system. It's why many people still swear on the *Holy Bible* before giving evidence in court.

The red covered 'penny' *Catechism* of childhood was another matter with almost 3,000 bite-size explanations for the *Ten Commandments* and the entire teachings of the Church. We would recite them in class and dread being asked by teacher, nun, or priest, to remember key ordinances by heart. It was God-by-rote and had very little meaning to me. My mind always went blank when questioned. But in my search for a way back, I stumbled across two rules of the road that had faded from my memory. In one of his theological duels with the legalistic Pharisees, Jesus said, 'You shall love the Lord your God with all your heart, and with all your soul, and with all your mind. This is the greatest and the first commandment. The second is like it: You shall love your neighbour as yourself' (Matthew 22:36-39).

There is much to ponder there. Reading those lines – straight from the mouth of the founder – was a key moment for me. I could feel the love pouring from those thirty-nine words. And wished with all my heart, my soul and mind, that I'd truly listened to them all those years ago.

These two rules of the road began to light my way home.

HEAVENLY CHECKLIST

I AM NOT SUGGESTING for a moment that there is a tick-a-box test for returning to the faith, a sort of re-entrance exam. Nobody has designed a faith-rating-scale for measuring the depth of an individual's religious commitment. Any 'testing' is a matter for discussion between God and each of us. But occasionally we may ask ourselves – as Catholics, just what do we believe in?

There is a checklist for this, one we recite out loud at Mass every Sunday and during the rite of baptism. The *Apostles' Creed*, a prayer whose roots traditionally stretch back to Apostolic times, in which we express our deepest beliefs about the Catholic religion. It is what we stand for and perhaps, at one stage, was a sort of extended password among persecuted early Christians.

As a faith formation aid in a time before the printing press, the creed's twelve articles of faith were learned off by heart, a tradition continued to this day. But just in case we have a memory slip, the creed is also screened on church monitors and printed on Mass cards.

I barely managed to remember the opening lines when I first began to think about returning to the Church. But looming panic faded when I googled God to rediscover this anthem of our faith. You'll find the creed below and you may want to linger over this ancient statement of belief for a while. You may want to think about the many millions of believers who, down the centuries, have prayed or sung these sacred lyrics in nations across the globe.

People have died for the right to make these declarations, affirming belief in the *Holy Trinity*, and seeking eternal life. But these hallowed verses also build bridges between the hearts of so many believers, with their mysterious cycle of love, death and hope. It may help you think more deeply about the faith by saying them slowly out loud in the privacy of your own home, or while walking in a peaceful place, or maybe silently when travelling on the bus or train.

They are words of deep commitment, presenting a personal covenant between us and God. In our rational age the creed is a challenging one. But as Christians we also live in a spiritual realm where not everything can be explained but anything is possible. At the core of this faith is our Christian belief in the Resurrection of Christ.

We cannot demand physical proof for ourselves as Thomas did. But he and most of his Apostle companions were later executed for preaching their eye-witness accounts of the life, death and resurrection of Jesus. They knew what they saw and could not wait to tell the world about it. And two millennia later, we echo their belief, one article for each Apostle. The creed was written about three hundred years after they died and, memorably, captures the holy essence of their teaching.

> *Today, we would probably call it their mission statement but one like no other.*

The *Apostle Creed*'s 12 articles of faith

1. I believe in God, the Father almighty, Creator of heaven and earth,
2. and in Jesus Christ, his only Son, our Lord,
3. who was conceived by the Holy Spirit, born of the Virgin Mary,
4. suffered under Pontius Pilate, was crucified, died and was buried:
5. he descended into hell; on the third day he rose again from the dead;
6. he ascended into heaven, and is seated at the right hand of God the Father Almighty;
7. from there he will come to judge the living and the dead.
8. I believe in the Holy Spirit,
9. the holy catholic Church, the communion of saints,
10. the forgiveness of sins,
11. the resurrection of the body,
12. and life everlasting. Amen.

A CHILD AGAIN

For Catholics, a ground-breaking practice to emerge from the COVID-19 lockdowns was the Church's official blessing to attend Mass online or 'join' a service on TV. Millions googled God and flocked to these digital pews. Perhaps some were potential returnees, unsure about attending the real event at a local church but interested enough to go to Mass in the sanctuary of their own home. During lockdown, I 'attended' Australian church services streamed online via local parish websites. I also went to Masses screened from America to experience the universal bond of our religion in this time of crisis.

But when I returned to the faith more than fifteen years ago, such internet services were not yet available. And I did not think to check my city's TV guide for screened Mass times. Watching a Mass on TV would have helped settle some of my nervousness about failing to attend Sunday Mass for decades. I had not even switched on a televised Mass at Christmas or Easter which many estranged Catholics nostalgically do to maintain a connection to our religion. But I was aware there had been major changes to the presentation of the Mass post-Vatican II.

When I left the Church, we were still reciting and singing the entire liturgy in Latin from dual language Mass cards and the priest – as noted earlier – stood with his back to the congregation. As a child, I had no concrete idea what the Church Latin words meant but they sounded sacred and mysterious.

I had never taken part in a Mass in my native language of English and no longer had any sense about when to stand, kneel or sit. Even more critically, I would not know what to say and when. I feared I would stick out like the proverbial sore thumb. This was all about me being too self-conscious and embarrassed. I did not want to make a fool of myself. I had not yet realised that humility, encouraged by Jesus, means parking your ego at the church's front door.

Falling back on my journalistic practice of doing the research before an interview, I decided to buy a Sunday missal to study the 'new' format. I went to a religious bookshop in the city and, after a little browsing, was drawn by one of those pocket Bible-size versions of the missal. They cover the order of the Mass and all sorts of religious texts including *Old* and *New Testament* readings for three years. But as I felt the weight of the book both in my hands and on my shoulders, I felt more than a little defeated.

Then I had a light bulb moment and went over to the children's section and found a much shorter, simplified version of the Mass book. It was a lot less expensive too! My first missal as a returnee was a simple, user-friendly child's copy. I was no longer quite so lost. I'd found the perfect guidebook.

> *In a sense, I was returning to the church in the best possible way, as a child again.*

DAY 13

A DIP IN THE DEEP END WITH GOD

Is it time to leave your comfort zone and attend your first Mass in years? It took me too long to make that decision. As I wrestled with God, or my emotions, I could not quite pluck up the courage to just go to a Sunday Mass in my parish. Instead, I waited till I was on a once-in-a-life-time holiday with my wife, 19,000 kilometres from our Sydney home to take that first step to Sunday Mass, through the doors of one of the world's most famous churches.

It was Notre Dame Cathedral in Paris which I had first visited a few days earlier, just like any tourist popping into a museum. I had done so with reverence, of course, just as I had when I walked into St Peter's Basilica in Rome a week before. It had not occurred to me to go to Mass in the Vatican's most famous church, the home of the Pope. And if it had, I would probably have told myself it would be said in Italian anyway. But suddenly in Paris as we looked down the central aisle to the huge altar, my Protestant-raised wife said, 'I think we should come to the service on Sunday'.

We were staying nearby, and I had no excuses to offer. On the Sunday, the cathedral was packed to the rafters for a special memorial service to commemorate the memory of those who had died fighting for the French resistance during World War Two. I watched a group of now ancient survivors carrying banners slow marched down the central aisle. And I could not help but shed tears at the sight of these old men and women who'd fought so bravely against tyranny when they were young. My father too had battled across France after taking part in the D-Day landings and was wounded in action twice, so he was on my mind as I finally prayed at a Mass.

The Mass was celebrated in French, of course, but I could follow the rhythms of the service and when came to Communion time, I felt saddened not to be rising from my kneeler and joining the long line to the altar. I had not been to confession for decades and I wasn't yet ready to make that commitment. But unlike the brave men and women being honoured that morning, I could feel my resistance beginning to crumble. I yearned for that holy wafer, but I still felt a certain spiritual disorder in my heart. I knew God would forgive me, but could I forgive myself for such long neglect of my soul? Which, when you think about it, was no way to think at all.

My wife said she wished I could have taken Communion in such a special place, giving me more spiritual food for thought. Early the next morning, I felt a compulsion to return to the cathedral. I dressed quickly and hurried across the already busy boulevard to the cathedral doors. It was not long after daybreak, but the doors were open in welcome. I stepped into the silence of the vast basilica, dipped my fingers in the font of holy water, blessed myself and saw I was virtually alone. The pews were empty, and I knelt in one about halfway to the altar where God is waiting to welcome us.

I prayed for guidance and then I heard a puzzling sound that seemed to be slowly moving down the dimly lit right-hand side of the church. The sound went clink, clink, clink. And for a fleeting moment, I wondered if there was a ghost in the cathedral, gently rattling their chains. Then passing like a shadow through an archway I saw the bent figure of an old man with a sack. Into which he was emptying those small tin votive candle holders whose flames had burnt out. As the clinking faded into the distance, I went over and lit a candle to Our Lady and the infant Jesus.

I no longer felt like a tourist. The candle's flame was flickering in my heart too.

TAKE THE WEIGHT OFF YOUR SOULS

WE HAVE NOW travelled two thirds of the way on our private pilgrimage. We can look back and ponder how far we have come in such a short time. But there is still a fair distance to travel, perhaps the hardest part of our inner *Camino* journey still lies ahead of us. Maybe it's time to take the weight off our soles and souls and contemplate a little on our lives since we were young, perhaps raised in very different times and places.

As a child of the faith, it had all looked so much simpler. Many of us did not really think too much about our religion at all. We may have knelt by the bedside to say our night and morning prayers; going to Mass on Sunday was a given and struggling to think of sins to list for the priest in the 'box of truth' was commonplace. We hot-footed past Protestant churches with the priest's warning ringing in our ears that even to peek through the doors guaranteed a swift descent to hell.

In those days, we did not hear much about the love and compassion of God, it was more about fire-proofing your soul against the flames of hell. But there was the magnificent mystery of it all; the mystical Latin, the ringing of the bells, the sacred hymns and the cloudy aroma of the burning incense that never quite fades from memory. And the great feasts of Christmas and Easter – the birth and the rebirth – that still draw millions of non-practising Catholics back through their parish church doors twice a year.

For most Catholic adults, the past isn't a foreign country at all. It is the land of nostalgia and it's where the seeds of our faith were first sown. Jesus famously told a parable about the seeds that failed, either falling through cracks in rocks, being choked by weeds, or unable to flourish in barren soil, while the seeds that thrived were growing in the right soil, the rich earth of faith. But maybe some seeds take a lot longer to deliver their fruits than others. And some weeds may be flowers in disguise.

I once liked to tell myself that I had turned my back on the Church and not on God. But one does not have meaning without the other. The bond is indivisible and invisible. The Church is filled with the Holy Spirit. It is the flower of our faith. Each Church is a sacred place, it is a little slice of heaven on earth. It's where the living body of Christ waits for us at the altar at every Mass. That is what I did not understand or appreciate as a child. It is why I now continue to make this inner pilgrimage every day.

We do not return just the once, but every time we make the sign of the cross, every time we think of him.

THE BREAD OF LIFE

B UT WHY AND WHEN did I seriously start contemplating returning to the Church? What was the turning point? When we're baptised as infants, we have no say in the matter; our parents sign us up for life and beyond in the Catholic Church. As a teenager I chose to quit the faith of my own free will. But now as I slipped into old age, was I taking out some insurance, some eternal life-cover for when I meet God face-to-face. In returning, was I hoping my soul might be as white as my hair at that fateful appointment?

Thoughts like these must have strayed through my mind at the time, but I don't specifically recall them. It was something much more intangible; I just felt a tugging at my heart and possibly my soul. I felt a growing doubt about having quit the Church in the first place, probably sparked by an emerging need for a spiritual direction to my life. In fact, I'd spent several years studying other forms of religion – non-Christian as well as Christian – and for a while had been attracted to Sufism, a poetically mystical branch of Islam that focuses on love and compassion.

But ultimately all roads seemed to lead back to our 2,000-year-old faith and the teachings of Jesus. Like most who return to the faith, I also hungered for the spiritual nourishment of the Eucharist, which is why that powerful word means 'thanksgiving'. My soul was starving. Sitting among the hundreds of people in Notre Dame cathedral that Sunday in Paris, I was one of only a handful who did not rise to receive Holy Communion: the bread of life. I hadn't been to Confession for forty years and so I was frozen to my seat.

I felt a deep pang in my heart though as I watched my fellow churchgoers make their way to the priests at the altar. Afterwards, Rosalie said, 'I felt so sad for you. It would have been so beautiful for you to receive Communion at this service'.

So, receiving the Eucharist and all that entails, eventually was high on my list of reasons for returning to the fold. But most of all, I wanted to be with God again. To be in his own home and to speak with him straight from the heart and with a relatively clear conscience.

In a very Catholic way, I wanted to tell him how much I loved him. But more than that, to show him too. However, I realise that for many who have fled the Church in recent times, it's not as simple as that.

> *A deep sense of betrayal and distrust has caused a new exodus from the pews, which is something I would like to consider next..*

DAY 16

GIVE GOD A SECOND CHANCE

IT IS NOT HARD to get hot-under-the-collar about a wide range of issues debated daily in the mainstream and social media. The arguments become even more intense if they spill over into our private lives. Controversial matters concerning the Church often create particularly heated disputes, with outrage expressed over Church teaching against contraception, divorce, sex without marriage, abortion, same sex nuptials and the priest's vow of silence over what he is told in the confessional. No matter how serious the crime, and even if the penitent is refused absolution unless they report their offence to the police, the priest's silence remains sacrosanct. Even if it means facing jail themselves.

There are also the burning issues of the continuing ban on women priests and the Church cover-up of paedophilia and sexual abuse in the ranks of priests who have taken promises of celibacy. As someone who was sexually assaulted by a stranger when I was nine-years-old, my heart breaks at what happened to so many innocent children at the hands of abusers they had trusted. I deeply hope these wounded survivors are being helped by expert counsellors and legal advisers as they seek healing and justice.

Their abusers are being pulled out of the shadows and sentenced in the criminal courts. The Catholic leadership is also on notice, standing under the stern gaze of a public who will never allow them to forget the crimes that brought the Church to its knees in shame. Even so, millions have quit the Church over these issues – many in angry protest and others as matters of conscience – feeling they could not in good faith continue practising as authentic Catholics. They felt it would be hypocritical of them to do so. And many potential Returnees may feel these are major stumbling blocks to returning home.

But strongly held views on controversial issues need not be a hindrance. When I worked in divided Ulster, the discussion of religion and politics in many social settings was often a no-no. Weapons were figuratively left at the door. I felt something similar about returning to the Church. I wanted to leave any loaded opinions at the door and meet with God in harmony. Some old-school, non-practising Catholics may also be faltering at the door, fearing they have broken too many rules and will not be welcomed back. The divine gift of conscience is not there to paralyse us with shame or indecision; its true role is to help us make the right moral choices. Whatever troubles us about returning may be calmed through interior discussion with God or resolved eventually through the Sacrament of Reconciliation.

But if I may suggest one thing, it would be to pray for anxiety and rancour to depart from your heart as you walk through the door. The Church is still filled with God's grace and goodness and, after all, he is the reason why we go to Mass. Give God a second chance. That is exactly what he wants to give to us. It's what the story of the *Prodigal Son* is all about. Jesus left this parable as a gift for every one of us.

We are all invited to the Welcome Home party.

SAINTS WITH BATTERED HALOES

WHEN THINKING ABOUT returning to the Church, does the subject of heaven play a part in your reflections? Or not at all? Personally, I do not recall thinking much about life-after-life, except Jesus clearly demonstrated there is one. I was more concerned about the here-and-now of returning. It appears I am not alone. In a widely circulating online list of the top ten reasons for returning to the faith, neither heaven nor hell are mentioned. Is this because we find dying a taboo subject best left until a later date? But, equally, isn't the major hope of living the Christian life the promise of eternal residence in heaven? Or is attempting to imagine life in paradise just too hard to picture? For many of us as children, it was all about sitting on fluffy white clouds while plucking harp strings and singing hymns. A sort of Walt Disney heaven really.

Jesus made it clear that a tangible heaven exists though, mentioning it seventy times in the Gospel of Matthew alone. Every Easter, we are also reminded that he promised the 'good thief' a place in paradise the day they were crucified, as well as earlier declaring his Father's mansion has many rooms. Nobody will be homeless in heaven.

I must admit I did not begin to give the subject serious thought till after returning to the Church, I began attending funerals in my parish for the first time in decades. These were often for elderly people I had grown to know and like while sharing a pew with them at Mass. I felt I was showing them respect and solidarity. It was at one of the funerals that I first heard that in the eyes of St Paul – thus the Church – all who arrive in heaven become saints, or 'holy ones'. This is one of the reasons why we celebrate the Feast of All Saints, those souls who are known and unknown. Priests often underline this point when they tell us every saint was once a sinner, and every sinner can be a saint.

One moment we are refugees from our past and the next we are probationary saints. There will be plenty of anonymous returnees with battered haloes up there. But imagine being in the same company as Mary, Joseph, Peter, Paul, Mary MacKillop, and Mother Teresa. They are heroes of our faith. Their life stories offer spiritual refreshment, inspiration and hope.

For example, my middle name is Vincent after the 16th century French champion of the poor, St Vincent de Paul. I did not give this a second's thought until I was about nine and my large family fell on hard times. Mum and Dad turned to the *Society of St Vincent de Paul* for help and their volunteers made sure we had food on the table and clothes on our back till Dad recovered his health and returned to work.

I never forgot this and when I returned to the faith, I joined the *Society* as a volunteer so that in a small way I could 'pay back' the help given to my family when we needed it the most. I was drawn by the *Society*'s ethos of offering 'a hand-up, not a hand-out'. If I make it through those fabled pearly gates, I will certainly be shaking St Vincent by that helping hand and thanking him for inspiring so many to support the millions in need of aid and compassion across the world.

But it could be a delayed encounter because there is that half-way house between earth and heaven called Purgatory. This is the state or place – according to Catholic tradition – where errant souls may go for spiritual rehabilitation or purging. Purgatory is not referred to specifically in the *Old* or *New Testaments* but is implied to exist.

The *Catechism of the Catholic Church* (1030) also states: 'All who die in God's grace, but still imperfectly purified, are indeed assured of their eternal salvation; but after death they undergo purification, so as to achieve the holiness necessary to enter the joy of heaven'.

As a returnee, I got a hint of what this might mean when I came back to the faith and virtually underwent a second rite of passage, as I sacramentally absorbed again what it means to reignite a loving relationship with God. Even how we receive Holy Communion had changed since I'd last knelt at the altar rail as a teenager. Like the priest, we now hold God in the palm of a cupped hand as we lift the wafer to our lips. He trusts us that much.

Here is hoping there's time-off for good behaviour.

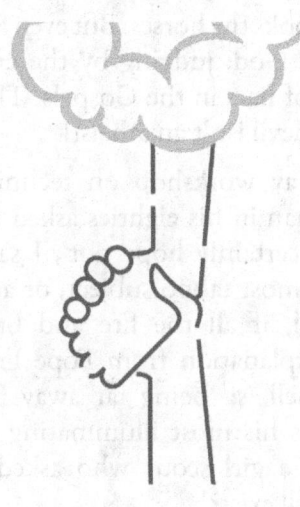

A MATTER OF CHOICE

Sometimes, we may complain that life is a living hell, or that we are trapped in a hellish situation. Often, we're talking about a job we loathe or a relationship that is failing. Not a place of fire and brimstone. But if we believe in Heaven and Purgatory, are we obliged to accept hell exists too? The Catechism – the Church's spiritual guide – states the answer is yes. But it is not a subject mentioned a lot from the pulpit these days, as ruefully confirmed by retired Pope Benedict XVI. In 2007, he said hell, 'really exists and is eternal, even if nobody talks about it much anymore'. It spooks the horses. But even Satan (which means adversary) believes in God, judging by the encounters between Jesus and the prince of liars in the Gospels. That is something to ponder, isn't it? The devil isn't an atheist!

I was at a one-day workshop on techniques of Christian meditation when a man in his eighties asked me: 'Do you think you'll go to hell?' 'I certainly hope not', I said. But he got me thinking about the almost taboo subject, or at least the sanitised version. What is hell, if all the fire and brimstone has been extinguished? One explanation from Pope Francis – Benedict's successor – is that hell is: 'being far away from the Lord for eternity'. But perhaps his most illuminating comment came in 2015 in response to a girl scout who asked: 'If God forgives everyone, why does hell exist?'

Acknowledging this as a 'good and difficult question', Pope Francis went on to describe a very proud angel who was envious of God: 'He wanted God's place. And God wanted to forgive him, but he said, "I do not need your forgiveness. I am good enough!".'

'This is hell', said Pope Francis. 'It is telling God, "You take care of yourself because I'll take care of myself"'. 'They do not send you to hell, you go there because you choose to be there. Hell is wanting to be distant from God because I do not want God's love. This is hell', concluded the Pope.

Other Church thinkers have speculated hell is empty of people's souls because once we encounter God in the afterlife, it is impossible not to believe in him. Or the love he offers us. As a late returner to the fold, I could be accused of taking out late-in-the-day-just-in-case heavenly insurance. But I love God with all my heart, all my soul, all my strength and all my mind. I also love my neighbour, difficult as that can be at times. I also believe that God cannot destroy what he has created. But if hell is a matter of choice, then I choose not to go there.

I'll be looking for the up elevator and I'm sure my guardian angel will be there to show me the way.

TRUE CONFESSIONS

I WAS KNEELING UNREPENTANT in the confessional the day I quit the Church all those years ago. I was angry with the priest who was prying too deeply into my moral lapses, minor as I believed they were. In truth, he was only doing his job, perhaps just a bit too fervently. But, as a headstrong teenager, I had not fully understood the priest is acting 'in the person of Christ' in the confessional. The compassionate face of Jesus is listening behind the screen. The priest was expressing his concern for the future of my soul.

I had not grasped that 'going to confession' is about remorse and forgiveness, not shame and punishment. But as I began thinking about returning to the Church, the relics of my teenage thinking still lingered. I felt highly anxious and ashamed about going to confession. I'd fallen from God's moral tightrope so often, how would I find a priest who'd have the time and patience to listen to a litany of failings longer than both my arms? But after prevaricating for about a year, I was walking past a city church one lunchtime when I felt a sudden urge to go in and make my confession. I had not yet spoken to a priest or any practising Catholic about my growing desire to re-join the Church. But I knelt in the waiting-pew alongside other penitents, said a prayer or two, and then sat back. I was happy to note that my thumping heart had settled back to normal. I felt at peace. I had a plan. I was not going to offer a grocery list of sins; I was going to express a dilemma. Then it was my turn.

I went into the room and the priest was sitting at a table with a lace curtain draped across the centre, shielding his face from mine. It was a substantial change from the dusty, wardrobe-size confessional boxes of my childhood. I knelt on a hassock on my side of the table and said, 'Bless me, Father, I have sinned. It has been forty years since my last confession'.

He murmured for me to continue, and I said, 'One of the reasons I have not been to confession is that after I left the Church, I married a Protestant girl in a registry office and...' I did not get the chance to continue. The priest had risen to his feet and stood looking down at me. Pointing a finger towards the door, he barked, 'Go – you know what you have to do!'

I was stunned. It was as though I had travelled forty years back in time and that the same priest was still shouting at me. I thought to myself, nothing has changed. More specifically, I had no idea what he was talking about. I hurried from the church, forgetting to genuflect towards the tabernacle, and out into the street in the sunlight and the noise of the traffic. Everything looked normal, but my world had turned upside down.

I walked along the hot pavement slowly, trying to collect my thoughts. I had rejected the Church and now apparently the Church was rejecting me. I did not know which way to turn. Slowly, I began to grow calm. I started to think about what the priest meant when he said: 'You know what you have to do'. Did he mean I had to go through official channels first and be guided by a priest back into the faith? But which priest? Certainly not the one who had just ordered me out of his confessional. I wondered to myself – where's Jesus when you need him. He would tell me what I needed to do next.

As I sat on the bus heading home, I prayed for inspiration. That night, after dinner, an idea suddenly struck me – google God. In the search box, I typed: 'Just tried to re-join Catholic Church by going to confession. Priest not helpful. What can I do?' Pages of results emerged seconds later. For example, if you type a version of that question in today you will get almost 17 million results in 0.62 seconds. The suggested links covered just about everything anyone needs to know about confession and it took me an hour or two to find a response that gave me the guidance I needed.

A post by a blogger revealed a similar encounter with a priest, but said he later found one who answered his prayers. The rescue-priest's name was Father Steve Curtin, and he was based in a Jesuit office in North Sydney. His office was only a few blocks away from where I then worked. Perhaps he would be the answer to my prayers too.

I rang Father Steve the next morning and explained my dilemma. He told me to pop into see him that afternoon. He was based in a Victorian terrace house. We sat in armchairs in front of a fire and he said I could make a general confession. I did not have to work my way through four decades of sins, but he did quietly ask if I'd ever murdered anyone. I was not surprised by the question because I'd worked in a country torn by religious warfare. My answer was a firm no.

Father Steve then gave me absolution and I said a prayer of penance. He also explained my marriage could be regularised by a special blessing ceremony called 'Convalidation'. This meant I would be able to fully take part in the sacraments of the Church again. He then smiled and said, 'Would you like to receive Holy Communion?' I said very much so.

After reminding me what my spoken response should be, he took out a small silver pyx, opened the lid and placed the host in my cupped hands while he said, 'Body of Christ' and I replied, 'Amen'. Father Steve then shook my hand and said, 'Welcome home, Bob'. And I burst into tears. My prayers had been answered. He also gave me a copy of the Bible. He said: 'I buy them at parish book sales for moments such as this'. I treasure this gift from Father Steve.

It is a source of great spiritual strength and insight and I try to reflect on a reading from the New Testament every day.

NO LIGHTNING BOLTS FROM THE PULPIT

It's almost the final day of our personal pilgrimage. Hopefully, it is time to take the plunge to attend Mass and receive Holy Communion in the company of fellow Catholics. You might feel exhilarated at the thought, or fearful, or even wondering – do I have the right to be there? Will I fit in? Will people know I am a returnee and think I am a counterfeit Catholic? A Prodigal slinking back, a stranger in my own house?

My mind whirled with all these emotions. But most of all – I felt confused. As I recalled earlier, the last time I had attended Mass as a practising Catholic was more than forty years ago. In those days, the entire Mass was spoken or sung in Latin, which I did not really understand but recited faithfully. The priest stood with his back to the congregation when celebrating Mass and we had knelt at the altar rail to receive Communion directly on the tongue.

Now, the Mass is said in the language of the country where you live or are visiting, while the priest faces the congregation. At Communion time, we bow in reverence as we approach the altar sanctuary and cup our hands like a chalice when receiving the consecrated wafer from the priest who says, 'Body of Christ' and we reply, 'Amen'. Although some people of all ages follow the old tradition and kneel to receive Communion on the tongue. Pre-COVID it had also become the practice to take a sip of the sacred wine from a chalice held by a waiting celebrant who said, 'Blood of Christ' and we replied, 'Amen'.

But most puzzling of all as a first-time returnee was this question: when do I kneel, stand, and sit during the service? Some priests will quietly say 'stand please' or 'kneel' or a cue may appear on the church projector screen which also displays hymns and Mass responses. But I copied what my fellow parishioners were doing until I felt more confident about the rites. You could also do some preliminary homework by watching a streamed Mass online or TV. One tradition has not changed: in most churches, there are two collections.

At my first Sunday Mass as a returnee, I sat at the back of the church in a pew with half-a-dozen other parishioners, all a similar age to me. At Communion time, I noticed several did not join the long queue to the altar. They were divorced believers hungering for spiritual nourishment but under Canon Law not able to receive the host or the wine. I shared the same spiritual hunger with them: they had come back to God too and were trying to get as close to him as possible.

I also discovered I was the only returnee in the congregation of about one hundred. Most of the parishioners had either remained faithful throughout their lives or were converts; or young believers, both single and married with children. The atmosphere was overwhelmingly welcoming. Many smiled at me as though I had been among their number for years. My fears of being an unwelcome stranger were groundless. The parish priest greeted me as if the forty-year absence had never happened. Shortly afterwards, he gave me a book of Jesus' most-loved parables to contemplate. 'There's always something new to think about', he said.

I also found a big change in the homilies. Lightning bolts from the pulpit are no longer commonplace. In their reflections today, many priests often like to use humour, draw parables from everyday life, emphasise the love of God, and occasionally share examples of wisdom from other faiths. One teaching story that resonated with me was related by a locum priest who told of two Buddhist monks on a pilgrimage walking from India to their monastery in China.

They came to a fast-flowing river which could still be crossed on foot. Standing on the riverbank was an attractive young woman who was afraid to make the crossing. So, one of the monks took her across the river on his back and said goodbye to her. The other monk had crossed the river in silence with him but now spoke up. 'Why did you do that? You know we are to have no contact with women. What if our brothers hear about this? It will cause great upset at the monastery'.

The monk who had helped the girl walked on in amiable silence, not replying to any of his companion's complaints and accusations. This did not deter the outraged monk, though, and for the next few hours, he shouted his charges repeatedly. But he was not getting a response from his friend who appeared to have taken a vow of silence over the matter.

Finally, the silent monk relented, stopped, and faced his accuser. 'I helped the young woman cross the river on my back and then put her down on the opposite bank" he said. 'This was several hours ago, but I note you are still carrying her.'

Our visiting priest was making the point that we often continue to carry in our hearts the rancour of a hurt caused by someone from a long time ago. We cannot find it in our hearts to lighten this burden by forgiving them and letting the matter go.

As I sat in the pew, I began to realise this was what was happening to me. I'd finally let go of the hurt in my heart. God had forgiven me and now it was time to forgive myself. It was time to let it all go. The Lost and Found Department had done its job. I now fully understood what Jesus meant when he told his Apostles: 'Peace, I leave you, my peace I give you'.

There is no other peace like it.

BACK TO THE FUTURE

Perhaps, like you, I was back where I began. A different church geographically but the same Church spiritually. The Pilgrimage of the Prodigal has reached its destination, or has it? I had gone from being a lapsed Catholic, to a returned Catholic and now a practising Catholic.

The Church is the Catholic faith. One does not exist without the other. And every day we can strive to live by the practices of our faith. Whether we succeed or not is another matter. We are not perfect, but we can seek guidance, strength and comfort through a prayer as simple and profound as the Sign of the Cross. It is how we stay connected to God and each other. It is how we can express our belief and love for the one God.

A small act of kindness is how we can express God's love for our neighbour, for each other. We are encouraged to go to confession and receive Holy Communion at least once a year, usually at Easter time. Once our marriage had been officially blessed by Father Steve through convalidation – a beautiful church ceremony with prayers and readings that lasts about half an hour – I decided to go to Mass every weekend. My wife, Rosalie, remains a Protestant but comes to Mass with me on special occasions and now most weekends with our younger daughter, her husband and our four young grandchildren.

True, the pews are no longer as full as they once were, but Mass at my parish church is the closest I will ever get to God in my lifetime. And I feel strengthened both spiritually and physically when I receive Holy Communion. It is a deeply sacred moment when the Bread of Life is placed in the palm of my hand by the priest, a fragile holy wafer that is true food for the soul. Jesus is my guest for the day.

There is the practical side of the faith too. Parish churches do not live by bread alone and volunteers are always welcome to share everyday duties, especially behind the scenes. This can lead to unexpected encounters. A man who was contemplating converting went to our parish church late one weekday morning in search of a priest to guide him. The place appeared silent and empty and then he heard a familiar sound out the back of the church.

He went out and saw a slightly built man sweeping the restroom floor with a broom. He asked him where the priest could be found? 'I am the priest', replied the cleaner. The man who was thinking of converting later said, 'A priest sweeping the restroom floor? I thought this is the faith for me. I asked if I could help him finish his chores'. And so, his conversion began.

There are other ways to help too. I took the plunge early and joined the *Society of St Vincent de Paul*, making home visits to help those in need of food, clothing, or furniture. You may recall that I did this because I remembered how kind *Society* volunteers were to my family when Mum and Dad were too ill to work. In the food on our table and the shoes on our feet I saw Catholic love in action, even if I was too young to recognise this at the time.

World Youth Day was held in Sydney for a week in 2008, the second year of my return to the faith, so I volunteered to help with crowd control. I wore the blue, yellow and red uniform on the bus while travelling from home to events and felt a little self-conscious until passengers began smiling creating an unspoken bond. I will never forget Pope Benedict's astonished face when he arrived by boat at Darling Harbour and saw the sea of happy young faces waiting to greet him. Their roar was deafening.

The city was almost crime-free for that week and the only hiccup I encountered was at the final Mass at Randwick racecourse.

In my section, some elderly churchgoers began pushing young people out of the way. They were in a hurry to receive Communion from one of the scores of priests on duty. A panicking priest said, 'Can't you control them?' So, I got the grumbling old ones back into line and a young woman shouted, 'Leave them alone, can't you?' Faith-wise, God was on a winning streak at Randwick that day.

But there was one rite of return I resisted for a long time. When I was a lad, I was told I had the face of a choirboy but the voice of a bullfrog. I was put in the school choir during an inter-school competition and firmly instructed to mime the lyrics only. Mum, who had been in my hometown's cathedral choir, agreed with the teacher's voice ban. 'You're as flat as a tack', she said.

I think this was why I had conveniently forgotten that going to Mass can require a fair bit of hymn singing, especially at Christmas with the carols. I kept my mouth firmly shut while longing to join those who were singing around me. Then one day a visiting priest began singing the *Our Father* and we all seamlessly joined in harmony. It was though we were singing with one voice and the moment felt deeply sacred and moving.

The next week, we were back to speaking the prayer Jesus created for us. I was acutely disappointed. It was then I realised that my pride was getting in the way and so I began to join in with the voices scattered around me during the hymns. As I croaked along, part of me stopped to listen to myself. I sounded terrible but I was beginning to enjoy the experience. I should have been embarrassed but I wasn't. Then I realised why I was not and felt a big bubble of joy in the middle of my chest. So, I cranked up the volume, even if I was flat as a tack. I was back in tune with God.

> *And if you have made our journey this far, I am sure you are in fine voice too – welcome home!*

21 Days Back to God

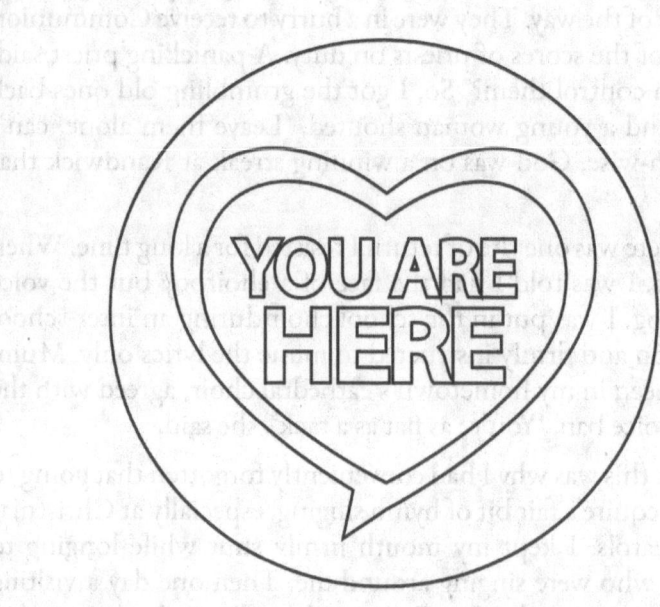

In my section, some elderly matriarchs began pulling young people out of the way. They were in a hurry to receive communion from behind the scenes of the altar. A panicky "pre-cantor" said, "Can we continue singing?", got the grumbling old encouraging flock and a young woman short call. Leave them alone can't you bah, please God: I was in a whirling mental whirlpool that day.

But there we stood, simply faithful, hanging in there. When I was a kid, I was told that God could hear the faint of the voice of a bullfrog. I just, I say, I just knew. In my little school, the computer taught Mass. He often made fun of the Our Father. I had thing to say, I was so little about it then. As I sat with the teacher, knew him. He was the first person there, he said.

I thought this was why I had been silently formulating that prayer. Was carrying the faint bit of body stepping up with a children's choir with the child. I kept my mouth firmly shut while longing to join those who were singing so beautifully. Then on, day's within, gift began singing the Our Father. And all at once I is joined in harmony to you. Though we were certainly a while the tone and the moment felt deep-seated and nervous. ???

The next week, as we were back to meeting, the prayer feast dragged on. I was mindfully appointed. It was then I realized that my grip was keeping in tune way and of less self. Look in with the voice surround rounding me during the hymns. As I croaked along, part of my stopped dreaming to myself. I sounded terrible. But I was beginning to enjoy the experience. I should have been able to speak if I had wanted. That I replied why I was not, and it is a big bubble of joy in the middle of my chest. So I cranked up the volume at it was. I was at last back. I was back in tune with God.

www.ingramcontent.com/pod-product-compliance
Lightning Source LLC
Chambersburg PA
CBHW012009090526
44590CB00026B/3935